It's
Wales

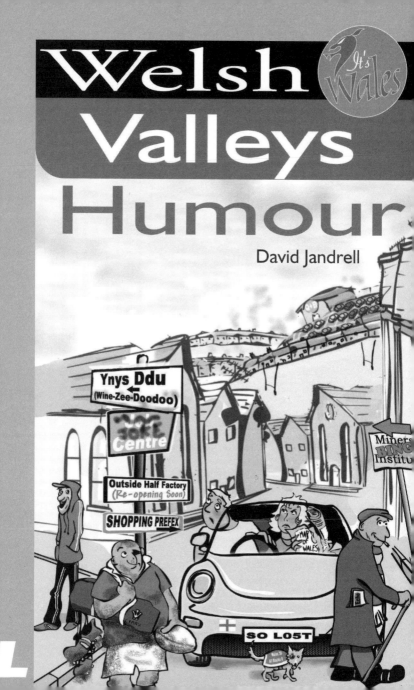

Cover illustration: Sion Jones

Cover design: Ceri Jones

Cartoons: Stuart Szymanski

ISBN: 0 86243 736 9

Printed on acid-free and partly recycled paper
and published and bound in Wales by
Y Lolfa Cyf., Talybont, Ceredigion SY24 5AP
e-mail ylolfa@ylolfa.com
website www.ylolfa.com
tel (01970) 832 304
fax 832 782

Contents

Foreword

English is a very funny language. The meanings of words and sentences can be very ambiguous. For instance, the first sentence above. Does the word 'funny' mean odd, or comical? When someone says, 'My cold is better', do they mean 'improved' or 'cured'? These ambiguities can lead to some very funny remarks. We are all familiar with the spoof advert 'For sale large chest, suitable for lady with roomy drawers.' This is simply words put in the wrong order – sometimes called a 'howler'. My daughter, when eight years old, wrote, 'The Titanic was a big ship that sank when it hit an ice-cube' (this was in my gin and tonic period).

The wrong word is always funny. Sometimes called 'malaprops', here is a true one spoken by Miss Joan Plowright, Lady Olivier – when a fellow-guest at a house party said she had brought no clothing suitable for a country walk, said 'Surely someone can lend you a pair of courgettes'. Courgettes, culottes, at least they are both French.

Perfectly straightforward statements can be misunderstood:

A yokel goes into a souvenir shop.
'I'd like a Union Jack, please.'
'Certainly, sir.'
'A green one.'

'There aren't any green ones, sir. They're red, white and blue.'

'Alright, I'll have a blue one.'

Aother yokel (to his yokel friend), 'You've got your shoes on the wrong feet.'

'These are the only feet I've got.'

I love this sort of joke. I find language so full of opportunities for humour; I loved the monologues I used to do on 'The Two Ronnies' – the man who used the wrong words (or worms, as he called them) and was consequently the spokesman for the Loyal Society for the sufferers of Pismonunciation; or the man who began every word with a W, and in the greengrocers asked for a wick of welery, a woocumber, two wackets of frozen weas and a walliflower.

The variety is infinite, the list endless. Words with two meanings; 'The policeman chased the thief past the butchers, past the bakers and caught him by the cobblers'. Silly sounding words, like 'auspices', and finally, my favourite of all, misprints. I have a collection of these, and they have made me laugh time and time again. 'Miss Tatiana Pushkin was the principal danger in the London Ballet Company.'

Words, words, words. What a delight; and what a delight David Jandrell's book is. He, like me, loves words, and finds them irresistibly funny. I hope you will too. I know you will. Take my word for it.

Ronnie Barker, 2004

Introduction to Valley Speak

A person entering the valleys for the first time will be subjected to a language that will, at first, be unfamiliar to them. An Englishman, or even someone from Cardiff, may experience difficulties in understanding parts of, or even everything a fluent Valley Talker may say.

This is a guide to the ways in which Valley Speakers use English, in the hope that by the end of this section, a visitor will be able to converse in the valleys, and will be approaching fluency in Valley Speak.

A valley person will not have any trouble understanding people who use Cockney, Geordie, Brummie, West Country or 'received pronunciation' (BBC) English, but people who use these accents or dialects will encounter massive problems when listening to a response in Valley Speak.

Valley Speak is a very parochial language and it is used by many thousands of people. It is not immediately identifiable to most English speakers, but can be spotted a mile off by people who live within a stone's throw of the valleys.

I have travelled into England on several occasions and spent a lot of time there. The reaction of the English to my accent was that I was obviously a Welshman. I picked up the usual nicknames such as 'Taffy',

Some people say it's easier to do this than understand 'Valley Speak'!

'Boyo' and even some 'sheep' references, the reason for which I am still at a loss to explain. Incidentally, I have never ever heard the term 'boyo' used in conversation in Wales. The only time I've heard it used is in England or on TV when people try to 'take off' the Welsh accent by peppering their sentences with 'boyo' and making sure that every phrase finishes with 'isn't it?'

The English were not able to be more specific about my accent other than it was Welsh, and I remember being on a field trip with two boys from Llanelli, one from Barry, one from Wrexham and two boys from Peterborough. To the Peterborough lads we all sounded the same, even though, within Wales, our accents were as diverse from each other as you can possibly get.

Whilst regional accents are quite common within Wales, the 'valleys' accent raises more eyebrows than most. In England my accent is Welsh, but in Wales I'm a 'valley boy', and my accent has been ridiculed and patronized more in Newport and Cardiff than anywhere else in the UK or abroad.

Being a fluent Valley Speaker myself, I have been able to identify certain areas which could cause confusion to the uninitiated. My training has been gained from more than thirty years as a resident in the Western valleys of Old Monmouthshire. Even though South Wales is made up largely of valley communities, there are several traits which appear to be common to all, from the Eastern Valleys to the Rhondda and everywhere else in between.

This work is not intended to be a crash course in linguistics or an in-depth study of grammar – it is merely an introduction into Valley Speak and it highlights certain areas of potential confusion.

A Rough Guide to Valley Speak Grammar

Double, triple, quadruple and even more negatives.

To the scholar of the English language, the double negative is severely frowned upon, and several examples can be brought to mind.

When I think back to my schooldays I can remember teachers becoming very irate when offered phrases like 'I didn't do nothing, sir' as an excuse.

The teacher would take great care to explain that the excuse contained a 'double negative', and that although the overall meaning was meant to convey that the child hadn't 'done it', what the child had *actually* said was that he/she *had* done it.

The double negative is also frowned upon in Valley Speak. Why use a double negative when you can use three, four, five, six, or seven negatives? The grammatical rule that governs this is the length of the sentence. The longer the sentence, the more you can chuck in – a very easy rule to remember and apply.

Case Study 1

A friend popped round to see me one evening. I offered him a cup of tea and he accepted the offer. After making the tea, I was just about to bring it in from the kitchen and I asked him if he took sugar. He said that he did, and when I visited the sugar bowl, I discovered that I didn't have any. When I broke the news, he responded with:

'I don't want no tea, not without no sugar anyhow.'

I knew exactly what my friend meant – 'if you haven't got sugar, I don't want the tea.'

I couldn't help wondering what a scholar of English would make of the statement; in particular if the scholar were to analyse it and try to decipher exactly what my friend had said.

Imagine for a moment, a retired army general moving to a picturesque village on the edge of the Brecon Beacons to experience the views and to open a quaint tea garden to make a few bob in the summer. Imagine the Oxbridge and Sandhurst educated gent watching my friend approach the counter, unaware that he is going to ask for a cup of tea, and also unaware that the warehouse has failed to deliver the sugar needed to replenish the stock which ran out on the previous day!

Case Study 2

'I don't want no tea, not without no sugar anyhow', actually contains five negatives. Another 'fiver' comes from a work colleague who decided to comment on the fact that I was eating a banana, by saying:

'They en no good to you, they don't do your indigestive system no good.'

I am assuming that the word 'indigestive' is a negative form of 'digestive' when used in conjunction with the word 'system'. The digestive system is widely regarded as the successful assimilation of food along the miles of tubing that we have inside us. An 'indigestive system' must, therefore, be the opposite.

The word **en** is also a negative and is explored fully below.

En, Ent and Tent

The advice about the adverse effect that bananas have on the digestive system mentioned above contains the word **en**. This is a very strange beast and deserves further study. This is a very common word in Valley Speak and it appears in a wide variety of forms and contexts.

The most common forms are and **ent**. They probably equate to the English slang **ain't**, meaning **it isn't**. Exactly when to use **en** and not **ent** and vice versa is one for the connoisseur, and the rules of grammar governing their usage are not clear. The fluent Valley Speaker will have this skill built in – I think there's a gene for it.

A typical conversation that will illustrate the different usages of the term would be:

> 'I en going to the party on Friday.'
> 'Why en you going?
> 'I just ent.'

The knowledge of the correct use of **en** and **ent** can only really be learned by speaking Valley Speak as a first language. It may not be prudent for the casual learner to attempt this but it is essential for those who intend to reside in the environment on a long-term basis. People who use **en** when **ent** is more appropriate may be identified as being 'not from round yer', and would be regarded as a 'learner' rather than using Valley Speak as a mother tongue.

Tent is another form of the word which could be regarded as a potential problem. The main drawback of this form is that the word also appears in English and has an entirely different meaning. **Tent** is usually used as an exclamatory term when the user wants to impress on another person that 'It isn't!'

In Valley Speak, **tent** is the shortened form of **it ent**. **Tent** can be shortened further to **ten**, as in the following conversation:

'Is that book yours?'
'Ten mine.'

Imagine for a moment a professor of English at Cambridge staying with friends in a valley village. The professor buys a paper from the local newsagents and notices that the route to and from the shop is tarnished with large piles of dog's mess. The professor notices a local walking his dog and says to him:

'I'm sure that your dog is the one that's fouling the public highway.'
'Tent!'

The professor will obviously be fully aware of the word **tent** and it's meaning. It would be interesting to have an insight into the professor's thoughts following such an incident, particularly as in response to an accusation that a person's dog was breaking the law, the owner retorted with a brief and curt reference to a canvas shelter, popular with people who favour camping holidays.

Generally Negative

We tend to speak a bit negatively in the valleys you know. Even though we may sound negative, we are actually being positive; we just prefer to sound as if we fear the worst, so if we don't get what we want, it's not such a let down.

An English shopkeeper may be confused; for instance, if a valley person went into his shop and asked, 'You haven't got any milk have you?'

A justified response to this question would be, 'Why, don't you want any?'

In fact, our valley person was actually asking if the shopkeeper *had* any milk.

In reality, any request for any item in any shop will contain the statutory introduction, 'You haven't got any' and finish with 'have you?' All shopkeepers should, on hearing this, concentrate on the middle section, which will contain the name of the item that the valley person actually wants and treat it as a request for that item.

We also speak negatively in general conversation. I overheard a mother telling off her son in a supermarket one day. Apparently, she'd spent most of her time looking for the lad as he'd wandered off and she couldn't find him. When she finally spotted him running around the aisles, she grabbed him and shouted:

> 'If you didn't keep running off where I couldn't see you, you wouldn't get lost!'

Another example of this style of speaking comes from two friends meeting in the street and having a chat. Dai and Maldwyn are discussing their holidays.

'So Dai, you en going to Porthcawl this year then?'

'No Maldwyn, it's Tenby we en going to, it was Porthcawl we never went to last year.'

Tidy

Tidy is probably the most versatile 'English' word used in the valleys, meaning anything but the literal English version, usually to describe the appearance of rooms.

To analyse this completely could fill the rest of this book, so below is a list containing some common examples to enable the reader to get a feel for the word and its use. The brackets contain the nearest English equivalents in the contexts in which they are used.

'Don't forget to talk *tidy* to your teacher when you get to school after.' (Respectfully)

'Whenever I ask you to do a job, you never do it *tidy*.' (Properly)

'I tell you what, you done a *tidy* job there.' (Good)

'Bob's got a new job, getting a *tidy* sum for it an' all.' (Large salary)

'Drive back out, and see if you can park it *tidy* this time. (Straight)

'That meal you cooked for us tonight was well *tidy*. (Very tasty)

'Look at her over by there, she's a *tidy* bit of stuff.' (Attractive)

'I didn't think I passed that exam but I done *tidy* in it after all.' (Passed it)

'The way you've decorated this room out is really *tidy*, fair play.' (Impressive)

Hopefully by now, you should have a tidy idea of how this word is used.

Do?

When valley people relate sequences of events to listeners, they use a rather unique way of expressing themselves. If people regularly go to the pub, play bingo, have a game of darts, and have pasty and chips from the chip shop on the way home, they would not say, 'I go to the pub and I play bingo, I have a game of darts and I go to the chip shop and have pasty and chips on the way home.'

They would actually say, 'I do go to the pub and I do play bingo and I do have a game of darts, and I do go to the chips shop and I do have pasty and chips on the way home.'

So, we don't just *do* things, we *do do* things.

In conversation, the **do's** are normally shortened to allow the speech to flow and not sound cumbersome in any way. Here the first **do** will become shortened to **d** and can be heard in utterances such as:

'I d'do this and you d'do that.'

Case Study 3

I was once called upon to 'translate' a phrase that had been used by a fluent Valley Speaker. The person who needed my assistance was a Cardiff boy, who was totally unaware of Valley Speak and had no concept of the grammar and syntax associated with it.

He had asked the advice of a Valley Speaker on how to grow runner beans and had listened intensely to all the instructions and the methods used for a successful crop. He admitted that he had understood most of the instructions, but had been totally floored by the concluding sentence that the Valley Speaker had used in his description of the best way to grow the beans. The sentence that had caused the confusion was:

'…and if you d'do what I d'do and you d'do it right, you'll be right. Right?'

This came perfectly naturally to me, but the Cardiff boy stated that if the 'runner bean king' had rounded up his instructions in French, his level of misunderstanding wouldn't have been any greater. At the time I was a little sad when I realised that the two men had resided no more than 18 miles apart all their lives, and this total lack of knowledge of Valley Speak existed to such an extent that I had to act as an interpreter!

If I'd thought of it at the time, I would like to have explained what the 'runner bean' man had said by saying, 'What he meant was that if you d'do what he d'do and you d'do it right, you'll be right. Right?'

It would have been funny I suppose, but it always seems to be the case, you can always think of something better to say when the moment has gone.

Anecdote

I have heard tell of a posh English gent who popped into a valley pub. He asked, 'Which is the quickest way to get to Cardiff from here?' The landlord thought for a moment and replied, 'Are you walking or going by car?' The posh gent replied, 'By car of course.' The landlord responded,: 'That's the quickest way.'

Time and Place (Now and There)

When we give people information in the valleys, we like to make sure that they are under no illusions about what we mean. People like to know when they will get something from us, they like to know what time we will arrive to meet them, and they will want to know where we'll be meeting them.

Of course the answer we will give them, regarding times, will always be 'Now.'

We will then qualify this further by adding a more accurate estimation of our arrival time as in:

'I'll be there now, in half and hour.'

Further examples would be:

'Your tea will be ready now, in ten minutes.'
'We'll have this done now, by lunchtime.'

As far as places are concerned, we like to be more accurate than to specify a place as just *there*. No, we will pinpoint the whereabouts of the object or place by using the term **by there**. When questioning someone as to the whereabouts of something, we are not content with merely asking where something is, we have to be even more specific by asking where the something is **to**. Notice all these points contained in the following conversation:

> 'Where's the cordless phone to?'
> 'En it over by there?'
> 'It was over by here, but now it ent, is it over by there?'
> 'Well it en over by here either.'
> 'So where's it to then?'
> 'Didn't you take it upstairs when you was talking to your mam?'
> 'Oh aye, I did. That's where it's to.'
> 'Go and fetch it down by here then.'
> 'Aye, I'll go and get it now in ten minutes.'

We simply *must* make ourselves understood, you see. We can, in the same sentence, use alternative words for the same item, just in case the listener is in any doubt as to what we are trying to say, as in,

> 'Whose coat's that jacket?'
> 'Are them shoes your boots?'

We are also very keen to be polite and to show our generosity. When one of my colleagues was eating a bag of sweets, another colleague asked if he could have one. As generous as ever, the sweet owner responded, 'Have two if you want one.'

And how more polite could this request to borrow a newspaper have been: 'Are you reading that paper you're sitting on?'

Weem

Another aspect of valley grammar worth mentioning is the 'm' suffix which is added onto certain words. In English, people may use the words **I am** as an introduction to a statement describing their well-being or an intention to do something. This has been abbreviated over the years to **I'm**. In 'Valley', we have taken this a stage further, as we have decided to tag this onto other 'person' words. For example, **they are** becomes **they am**, abbreviated to **theym**; **you are** has become **youm**; and **we are** has become **weem**. A typical conversation containing examples of all these would be:

> 'I'm going down the Rugby Club on Saturday.'
> 'Tidy. Weem going down there, so if youm going, we'll see you there.'
> 'Is Bob and Mike going and all?'
> 'Aye, theym going too.'
> 'See you there, then.'
> 'Aye.'

Oven

A domestic scene.

> 'Oven the kettle boilt yet?'
> 'No it ovent.'
> 'Why oven it?'
> 'Because I oven put it on.'
> 'Why oven you?'
> 'I didn't know you wanted it on.'
> 'Well we oven had a cuppa yet.'
> 'Do you know where the kettle is to?'
> 'Aye, it's over by there?'
> 'Well put it on yourself then!'

> **Language Crossover**
> Be careful to avoid confusion with the word 'oven' here. There is an English word that is spelt and pronounced the same, but has a different meaning. Something to do with cookery, I believe.

Putting it all together

Now is the time to 'have a go'. The best way to learn a new language is to get involved in conversation and look out for the points we've learned so far.

Asking For and Giving Directions

If lost in the valleys, asking for directions can be a torrid affair.

A person who intends to ask directions will encounter several problems that could be minimised by following the pointers set out below.

Pronunciation

The pronunciation of Welsh place-names has been a source of confusion to strangers throughout history. The visitor to the area will be confronted with road signs and map references containing words that are half a yard long, most of which will not contain vowels, as they know them.

I remember being stopped by a courier who was on his way to deliver a parcel to Ynysddu, a village not more than four miles away from the point that he had stopped me. The correct pronunciation for Ynysddu is 'Un-Iz-Thee.' The courier asked me for directions to a place called, 'Wine-Zee-Doo-Doo.' I was initially at a loss to identify this as any place that I'd heard of, but all was revealed when he showed me the delivery note. I was able to direct him to Ynysddu with no problems.

Difficulties occur when people ask directions of a crowd of people. The best advice to those who would ask a group of locals, particularly

'I just don't know which way to turn!'

youths, is to ensure that their pronunciation is spot on. Any deviation from the usual will be greeted with furrowed brows until such time as one member of the group realises what is trying to be said. This person will then announce, 'Oh, you mean… (correct pronunciation)…' which in turn, will lead to extensive bouts of hilarity amongst the rest of the group.

It is vital therefore, that visitors learn how to ask for destinations in the local tongue if they want to avoid being laughed at and openly ridiculed until they finally drive off.

Local Terms

Every village has a landmark or area which has a 'name' that is exclusive to that village.

A common valley landmark is the Miners' Institute. Every village will have one. They are usually large buildings, which were widely used in the days when coal mining was rife in the valleys. Miners used these buildings as meeting places and they contained such facilities as libraries, snooker tables, dance halls etc. Nowadays, they are used for mother and toddler groups, bingo, community education and anything else that the locals can think of. These Miners' Institutes are usually the largest buildings in villages and there should be no confusion in identifying them when included in directions. Not so! This is because Miners' Institutes throughout South Wales are known as 'Stutes'.

If a village has a Co-op Store, this can also be a source of great confusion. Co-ops are known as 'Cworps' in the valleys, and I sympathise with a visitor who may ask for the whereabouts of the local post office and is told,

'Go straight down here till you get to the Stute, turn left and it's opposite the Cworp.'

There is a hill that leads from my village into the next village. The hill is known as 'Factory Trip'. The term Factory Trip will not appear on any map or road sign, but every villager will refer to this hill (officially called Twyncarn Road) as Factory Trip. Someone from the villages either side of mine will be totally unfamiliar with this local name, but I can guarantee that any person who asks for directions to get to a place which is south of the village, will be told to, 'Go straight down Factory Trip and turn either right or left.'

If I had been given a pound every time I'd heard this instruction given to a visitor, I'd be living in luxury in a beach mansion in the Bahamas by now.

Local Knowledge

A visitor may also like to bear in mind that a local will assume that a person asking directions will already have a vast knowledge of local geography at his/her disposal, and will use this supposed knowledge when giving the best route to a destination. The local will incorporate this technique alongside the use of local terms to ensure that the directions are as muddled as possible, making it essential for the visitor to stop and ask for updates from passers-by at least sixteen times for every half a mile travelled.

Try this:

'You know the roundabout by Evans's, well go straight over there as if you were going to the farm – not the big one; the small one where they had the fire, and then branch off left and it should be straight in front of you, unless the roadworks are still there and if they are you'll have to go right to get to it. You can't miss it anyway, it's in between the Stute and the Cworp.'

Case study 4

The best or worst (depending on your viewpoint) directions that I was ever given came as a result of asking directions in a valley that I was unfamiliar with when I was going to buy a guitar that I'd noticed for sale in the local Ad Mag. I had asked to be directed to a particular street and was told to:

> 'Go straight down here, go straight down through and then carry on going[1]. When you've got there[2], you'll see a road in front of you going off left. Take the other one after that[3] and go straight on. Then turn right before you get to[4] where the bus shelter used to be[5].'

Let's look more closely at these directions and see if we can identify possible areas of confusion.

1.   This has been split into three phases – 'straight down here', 'straight down through' and 'carry on going'. How does the visitor know at which point he/she has completed the 'straight down here' bit and moved into the 'straight down through' bit before continuing with the 'carry on going' part of the journey?

2.   Where is 'there' and how does he/she know when they've reached 'there'?

3.   Where is the 'one after that' in relation to the 'one going off left'?

4.   To instruct someone to turn off *before* they get to a landmark is not a particularly good practice. However this is not insurmountable. When given directions such as 'Turn left before you get to the filling station', the person who is lost must reach the filling station before realising that he/she should have turned off before reaching it. In this case, the problem can be overcome by turning round and going back to the required turning.

5.   If a person insists on using the 'Turn off *before* you get to the…' technique, it is vital that he/she makes sure that the landmark is still there. In this case, turning off before you get to where the bus shelter 'used to be', is of little help to the visitor, as he/she will now have to find out where the bus shelter used to be before proceeding.

In this particular case I resorted to using another technique which I have also heard when asking for directions, 'Well if I was going there, I wouldn't start off from here. The best thing you can do is go down there and ask someone else.' That's what I did.

By far, the most bizarre instructions that I have ever witnessed were those given to a person who wanted to visit a company that I worked for. I overheard a telephone conversation that was concerned with giving a customer directions to the company's premises. The best way to report this is to reproduce the conversation verbatim here: 'Well,

I'm not very good at geography so you'll have to bear with me. Now, where are you coming from? Airdrie, right… er do you know the lights in Crumlin?'

Airdrie is a town in central Scotland, between Edinburgh and Glasgow, and it seemed strange to me that the person giving the instructions should have deemed the first notable landmark between the two places as being the 'lights in Crumlin'. I would imagine that it would be difficult to find someone in Newport who would be familiar with these, let alone someone intent on travelling to the South Wales valleys from Scotland!

Here, the person giving the directions has decided to omit details of any major cities or motorways, in fact, he has even missed out an entire country! I would imagine that if there was a prize for the sparsest directions ever given, this particular incident would be a major claimant for the award.

Deliberate misdirections (for the English only)

A person who stops someone in the street and asks for directions in a strong English accent is liable to be subjected to another technique used by most valley people. This is the technique of giving perfect directions in a clear manner, containing no difficult words or local terms, usually to a destination in the opposite direction to the place that the English person wants to go.

This can be compounded when the English person follows the directions to the letter, arrives at the new destination, realises that he/she is *still* lost and asks another valley resident for directions. In this situation, it is quite possible for the visitor to end up farther away from their destination than they were before they left home.

Conclusion

When going to a particular place in the valleys, make sure before you leave that:

· You can pronounce the name of the place you wish to go to perfectly

· You know the area as well as a local person

· You learn all of the 'pet names' for local landmarks for all the villages in the locality

· You don't get lost

· If you do get lost, ask at least ten people for the same directions and then take a consensus of the answers before setting off.

Valley Jokes – Stories Depicting Valleys Life

Village life

To the outsider, village life will appear to be drab, boring and unfulfilling. This is a myth. Each village will be a hornets' nest of activity and gossip, and there'll be plenty going on, as long as you know where to look, and who to speak to.

Everyone will know everybody else's business. In fact, everyone has the right to know everyone else's business, and woe betide anyone who thinks otherwise. If someone goes into the pub on a Friday night with a new pair of socks on, by 10 a.m. on Saturday morning, everyone will know about it. The owner will be stopped in the street and quizzed about where did he get them from, how much they cost, what has he done with his old ones… and so on.

There are no secrets in the valleys, that's for sure…

One morning, as Evan was on his way to the paper shop, he was approached by a stranger; a shady looking fellow. The stranger spoke to Evan in a strong Eastern European accent. He said, 'I am lookink for Dai.' Evan thought for a moment and replied, 'Dai the milk?' The stranger said, 'No, no, it is Dai that I am lookink for.' Evan replied, 'Dai the bread?' The stranger sighed and said, 'No, please listen to me,

I vant to speak to Dai.' Evan replied, 'Dai the coal?' The stranger whispered into Evan's ear, 'The sun shines brightly over the meadow in summertime.' To which Evan retorted, 'Oh, you mean Dai the spy – he'll be down the club by now!'

* * *

In another village there lived a retired army colonel who had fallen in love with the Welsh scenery as a young man and decided to live in the valleys for the rest of his days. He had been accepted by the locals even though he was English and fitted into village life well. One day, he was pruning his roses and the vicar spotted him and went over for a chat.

'Good morning, Colonel. How are you today?'

'Fine thank you, Vicar, and you?'

'Excellent, Colonel. How long have you been in the village now?'

'Fifteen years, Vicar, and loved every minute of it.'

'In all that time, I don't believe we've seen you in church yet. Any reason for that, Colonel?'

'A very good reason, Vicar. I am an English speaker, and your services are conducted in Welsh.'

'Ah, but the collection is conducted in English, Colonel!'

* * *

Mrs Jenkins was very pleased when her son, Will, announced that he was seeing a girl from the village. She had been a bit concerned, as until the age of 23, Will was only interested in playing with his computer and she was beginning to have doubts about him. After the couple had been courting for six months, Mrs Jenkins decided to try to find out exactly how serious the relationship was. She sat him down after tea one day and said, 'How's it going with your girlfriend Will? Have you… er… you know, done it yet?' Will looked shocked and replied, 'No Mam, we haven't. You see, she told me she was a virgin.' On hearing this, Mrs Jenkins became very agitated and shouted, 'Will my boy, get rid of her! She en no good to you, being a virgin!' Will turned to his mother and said, 'But Mam, what's wrong with being a virgin?'

Mrs Jenkins replied, 'If she en good enough for the rest of the boys in the village, she sure as hell en good enough for you!'

* * *

When her husband died, Mrs Pryce-Jones spent the whole of the insurance money on a facelift, liposuction and a month in Bermuda. When she came back, she was very proud of her new appearance. She was tanned, her body was lithe and she looked like a film star. She decided to show herself and strode into the butcher's shop. After she had paid for her order, she challenged the butcher to guess her age. The butcher looked her up and down and guessed that she was 35. Chuffed to beans with this, she told him that she was older and asked him to guess again. This time the butcher guessed that she was 40. Over the moon with this, she proudly announced that she was actually 54. The butcher congratulated her on her looks for a woman of her age and she proudly left the shop.

A little later she spotted an old man hanging around outside the post office. She challenged him to guess her age. The old man looked at her and agreed to guess her age, but added that he'd have to conduct a few tests before he guessed how old she was. She agreed to the tests and was surprised when the man told her to loosen her clothing. Immediately, the old man put his hands inside her clothes and began groping her. After about 20 minutes, the man – who by this time was very hot and bothered – removed his hands and said, 'Madam, unless I am mistaken, I would say that you are 54.' Mrs Pryce-Jones was staggered at this announcement and asked the man how he could have possibly guessed her age correctly. The old man replied, 'Easy, missus. I was standing behind you in the butcher's.'

Rugby

Rugby has always played a big part in Welsh valley life. This game will be regarded as the most important thing in a village. All the local lads will be encouraged to play, and the Rugby Club will be the centre of the social life in the village. The doors will be open seven nights a week, catering for activities such as darts, pool, cards, dominoes, bingo, pigeon clubs... oh, and rugby. Any special social occasions will take place in the club. Birthdays, kiddies' discos, engagement parties, funeral wakes, and weddings will have the exclusive use of all the facilities, including the spacious car park which can double up as a handy place to 'fool around' with someone else's spouse, whilst at the same time being able to accommodate a brawl of anything up to 40 people. This facility is usually very popular following wedding receptions. These brawls normally start between the families of the bride and groom, but will include everyone on the guest list, including the bar staff and groundsman, by the time the police arrive.

There is generally a slight interest in the rugby team itself, with a few stalwarts who watch every game come rain or shine. The big events come during the Six Nations Championships. This is usually associated with trips to watch these Internationals, and more importantly, the away games!

Here are some tales that have filtered back to villages following these trips, and I am told that they are accurate representations of the things that have happened.

On the way to Twickenham one year, a crowd of England fans who were travelling to London from Cardiff were surprised when they saw six Welsh fans buy one ticket between them. The English fans asked the Welsh boys how they expected to get away with only buying one ticket for six people. One of the Welsh boys turned to them and said, 'Watch and learn'.

The English fans watched the Welsh boys cram themselves into the toilet on the train and realised the scam when the ticket inspector banged on the door saying, 'Ticket please'. After a while, the door opened slightly, and just one hand, clutching a ticket poked through the gap. The ticket inspector took the ticket, and went off happy.

After the game, which Wales won, they all met on Paddington station and the English boys were seen buying just one ticket, as the Welsh boys had done on the way up. The English were surprised when the Welsh boys didn't buy a ticket at all. They asked the Welsh boys how they expected to get all the way back without a ticket. One of the Welsh boys turned to them and said, 'Watch and learn'.

As soon as they got on the train, the English lads piled into the toilet, and two minutes later, one of the Welsh boys banged on the door and said, 'Ticket please'.

* * *

A very famous and prolific Welsh rugby star died and arrived at the Pearly Gates.

He approached the Saint who beckoned to the rugby star to enter the Kingdom of Heaven. The star looked a little sheepish and seemed reluctant to enter, which prompted the Saint to ask if there was a problem. The rugby star told a heart warming story: 'Years ago, we played England at Twickers and we were losing with a minute to go. I intercepted a pass in their half of the pitch and I ran like the wind down the wing and I scored a try in the corner. We won by one point. The thing is, just before I went over the line, I put a foot in touch. The touch judge didn't notice it and neither did the ref. I was going to

'Well why not, eh? If he can go all the way to Scotland to watch a blinkin' rugby match...'

own up, but when I looked up and saw all the Welsh boys on the terraces going crazy, I didn't have the heart to come clean and tell the ref that I'd scored an illegal try. This has been on my mind ever since. I feel really guilty that I didn't own up and I don't think that I am worthy to enter the Kingdom of Heaven.'

The Saint thought for a minute and said, 'Well, it looked like a perfectly good try to me and as far as I'm concerned you are welcome to come in.' The rugby star was over the moon and shook the Saint's hand as he entered saying, 'Thank you St. Peter, I bow to your generosity and I will be eternally grateful to you.' The Saint replied, 'Don't worry about it. By the way, I'm not St. Peter, it's his day off – I'm St. David.'

* * *

This story tells of another rugby legend – Barry John. Barry had gone to London on the night before a match between England and Wales at Twickers, to speak at a Rugby Club pre-match dinner.

He made his own way to the ground on the morning of the match and went into the dressing room and got changed. He was surprised to find that the rest of the Welsh boys weren't there. He got news that the team coach had broken down on the M4 and a replacement had been sent from Cardiff to pick them up and take them to Twickenham.

It was five minutes before kick-off time and the ref came into the Welsh dressing room for an update on the problem. Barry told him that the boys were on their way and asked if the England team wouldn't mind waiting for them to arrive.

The ref went to the England dressing room and came back with the news that they wouldn't wait and insisted that the game started on time. So, Barry had to go out and face the English on his own.

Outside the ground, there were about 20 Welsh boys who didn't have tickets, and a few lads from the Rhondda who were in the stand were shouting out to these lads what was going on. Ten minutes into the game, a huge roar went up. The boys outside shouted to the Rhondda boys asking what had happened. The Rhondda boys replied, 'Barry's just scored.'

*   *   *

A similar thing happened in a soccer match between Wales and England at the Millennium Stadium. All the Welsh lads went out for a few pints the night before the game and on the day they were severely hungover. Ryan Giggs, who hadn't been out with the lads the night before, was as bright as a button. The rest of the team really didn't feel like playing and asked Giggsy if he'd go out to face them on his own and they'd join him when they'd come round a bit. So, off Giggsy went to face the foe by himself.

At half time, Giggsy came into the dressing room and announced that he was 2–0 up.

The rest of the lads were still feeling rough so they asked him if he wouldn't mind playing the second half without them.

After the game, Giggsy came back into the dressing room in tears claiming that he'd let everybody down.

When they asked him the final score, Giggsy said he'd drawn 2-2 with the English.

The Welsh boys said that he'd done fantastically well, bearing in mind that he'd taken them on by himself, and by no means had he let everybody down. Giggsy replied, 'Oh, I did let everybody down, I got sent off ten minutes into the second half.'

*   *   *

Evan had saved a fiver a week for two years at the rugby club for the Twickenham trip. The time had finally arrived, and the coach left for London at 6 a.m. on the Friday before the game.

Evan got so drunk on the Friday night that he slept in and missed the rest of the party leaving the hotel for the game on the Saturday morning.

He decided to find his own way to the ground and found himself lost in central London with only an hour to go before kick off.

He spotted a city gent, dressed in a pin stripe suit and bowler hat on the other side of the road. He shouted across to the gent, 'Oi butty, where's Twickers to?'

The gent stopped, and looked aghast at Evan before replying.

'Actually old chap, you should never end a sentence with a preposition.'

To which Evan retorted,

'Fair enough – where's Twickers to, you stuck up twit?'

Farming

The huge rolling hills and mountains of the valleys play host to many farms. The farmers are very rarely seen in the 'lowland' villages, and villagers are not always welcome visitors to farms – unless the purpose of their visit is to hand cash to the farmer. Farmers will exchange virtually anything for cash – usually fruit, veg, eggs, manure, you name it. If the farmer has something you can use, he'll sell it to you.

They are quite interesting characters as they are so rarely seen, but every village will have a farmer residing high above them, and here are a few favourite stories concerning our elusive friends.

There had been a disaster on Dai's farm. The tractor had broken down and Dai was under pressure to plough his field to plant the next season's produce. Dai phoned a tractor engineer and agreed to pay the extortionate call-out fee.

When the engineer arrived, Dai told him that the tractor had broken down in the top field and it was still there. The engineer got in his car to drive to the top field. To get to the field from the farm entrance was a primitive road track, halfway along which was a ford stretching right across it. The engineer drove up to the ford and looked into the water. To be on the safe side, he asked Dai if it was OK to drive through it. Dai said it was no problem to drive through the water.

The engineer got back in his car, drove through and found that it was 17 feet deep!

He managed to crawl through the driver-side window and swam to the surface. When he finally dragged himself out onto dry land, he turned to Dai and said, 'I thought you said it wasn't deep!' Dai looked at the engineer and said, 'Well, it only comes halfway up our ducks.'

*   *   *

Dai and his son, Ieuan, had just ploughed a field and were heading back to the farmhouse for their dinner. They pulled out of the field, without looking to see if there was any traffic coming, right into the path of a Porsche that was travelling at about 80mph down the lane which bordered their field.

Going too fast to stop, the Porsche driver turned the wheel and went straight through the hedge into the field. The driver lost control of the vehicle and zigzagged across the field, completely destroying all the work that Dai and Ieuan had just done. Finally, the driver gained control, and steered the vehicle through the hedge on the other side of the field, got back on the same road further down and sped off.

Dai and Ieuan had watched all this from the cab in the tractor, and when the Porsche finally disappeared from sight, Ieuan turned to Dai and said,

'Bloody hell Dad, it's a good thing we got out of that field when we did!'

*   *   *

Dai met Will at the farmer's market one day. Dai was looking for a boar to 'service' his sows, hopefully to get a good litter of piglets to sell at next year's market. Dai had not seen a boar anywhere in the market and was going home disappointed.

Will told him of an old trick that his grandfather had taught him. He told Dai that he used to 'service' the pigs himself as pigs and humans were compatible and it was possible for a man to impregnate a female pig. He added that when the pigs had 'caught' they lay on their backs and waved their legs in the air.

Dai got back to the farm and loaded all the pigs into his van and took them to the remotest field on the farm. When he got them there, he 'serviced' them himself and drove them back to the farmyard where he put them back in the sty. He checked their behaviour the next morning and they were acting normally, so he piled them back in the van, took them up to the field and serviced them again. This went on for about three weeks, and Dai was getting pretty fed up with it – until one morning.

Dai's wife was up before him, and she came rushing into the bedroom shouting, 'Dai, quick wake up! Look out of the window and have a look at our pigs!'

Dai opened one eye and said, 'Don't tell me, they're all lying on their backs waving their legs in the air?' To which, Dai's wife replied, 'No, they're all sat in the van, tooting the horn.'

*   *   *

An American holidaymaker was driving through rural Wales on a sightseeing tour when he espied something very strange. He stopped the car and approached the thing that had attracted his attention – a chicken pecking away at the roadside, that appeared to have three legs! When he got near, the bird looked up and took off like the wind. The American had never seen anything move so fast!

He jumped into his vehicle and set off in hot pursuit. His car was going flat out to no avail. As he drew close, the chicken accelerated away and was soon out of sight.

Not satisfied with this, the American continued the chase until he came to a fork in the road. He stopped the car and got out and tried to decide which road to take.

Then he saw a farmer leaning up against the hedge. He asked the farmer if he'd seen a three legged chicken running down the road. The farmer said that there very possibly was a three-legged chicken on the loose as there were hundreds wandering the roads in the area. The American was shocked by this statement and asked the farmer how this could be. The farmer said that he'd been breeding three-legged chickens for years to sell to families of three people who all liked a leg on a Sunday for the traditional roast.

The American asked the farmer what they tasted like. The farmer replied, 'Dunno mate, we haven't caught one yet.'

* * *

Two young ladies of ill-repute were driving around rural Wales looking for men to have their evil ways with. They were deep in farming country and they spotted a burly, bronzed and muscular farmer leaning up against a farm gate having a fag.

They stopped the car and approached the farmer. The farmer eyed them up and down and assuming they wanted to ask directions said, 'Can I help you?'

One of the girls said, 'Hopefully, we need a good seeing to.'

The farmer took a big drag from his fag and replied, 'So do I – I just ploughed the wrong field.'

Tom, Dick and Harry Williams were, by far, the largest boys in the village. They were the sons of farmer Dewi Williams, a huge man who had farmed the hills for over 30 years. Tom and Harry were twins, both standing over seven feet six and weighing 25 stones, with not an inch of fat on them.

Dick, their big brother, was getting on for eight feet tall and weighing in at 30 stones, again without an inch of fat.

Tom and Harry went into town one day to buy new shoes. The woman in the shoe shop was amazed when they asked her for size 20 shoes, and said that in 40 years in the business she'd never seen feet as big as theirs. To which Tom retorted, 'If you think our feet are big, wait till you see the size of our Dick's!'

* * *

A man was driving home through a country lane when his car broke down. He peered under the bonnet and wondered what he could do to get it going again. He heard a voice behind him say, 'Give the petrol pump a tap, it should clear it.'

Without turning round, he tapped the petrol pump and tried to start the car. It started first time! He got out to thank the 'voice' and was staggered when he saw a horse looking at him from behind a hedge.

He couldn't see anyone near, so, a little puzzled, he got into his car and drove off.

A bit further down the road, he spotted a farmer and stopped. He told the farmer that he'd broken down and he thought that a horse had told him what to do to repair his car.

The farmer asked him if it was a brown horse that had given him the information. The man confirmed that it was a brown horse that appeared to have spoken to him. The farmer replied, 'Aye, well it's a good job it wasn't the black one, he don't know nothing about cars.'

* * *

Reg the farmer had been advised to take a holiday by his doctor. Reg agreed that he could do with a break, but was loath to leave the farm as the only person that would be in charge when he was away was Tom, a farm labourer. Whilst Tom was a first class worker, he was a heavy drinker, and when he'd 'had a few' he was totally useless.

Reg's wife spoke to Tom and made him promise that if they went away and left him in charge that he wouldn't touch a drop until they came back. Tom promised that he'd spend two weeks off the booze and make a good job of looking after the farm.

When they got back, Tom picked Reg and his wife up from the airport. As they were driving back to the farm, the conversation went like this:

'So Tom, how have things been since we've been away?'

'Had a few problems, Reg.'

'What sort of problems?'

'You know Shep the sheepdog?'

'Yes, of course I do.'

'Well, he's dead.'

'Dead! What happened?'

'He ate horse meat that had gone off.'

'What horse meat?'

'Oh, the horse is dead as well.'

'How come?'

'He died in the fire.'

'What fire?'

'Oh, the barn burned down.'

'How did that happen?'

'It was a spark off the farmhouse.'

'What?'

'Oh the farmhouse burned down as well.'

'How did that happen?'

'Struck by lightning.'

'Hang on a minute, have you got any good news for me?'

'Yes.'

'What's that then?'

'I haven't had a pint for a fortnight.'

Mining and New Industry

The Welsh valleys are famous for the coal that it produced during the times when mining put the food on the tables of most of the people who lived in them.

Coal mining has now almost died out, and unemployment has increased steadily in these once thriving areas. The pits were not very nice places to work, and many men lost their lives at work and many suffered terrible injuries as they went about their everyday duties.

This story tells of just one incident.

One miner had been trapped underground for some time, and was rescued, brought out unconscious and taken to hospital. When he came round, a doctor was sitting at his bedside.

'Mr Jenkins, I have some good news and some bad news for you.'

'Tell me straight, doctor.'

'I'm sorry to have to tell you, but you'll never work down the pit again.'

'And what's the bad news?'

* * *

Today most of the pits are gone. Also all the evidence of where they once were has disappeared under landscaped industrial estates. These small units provide work for the valley people and much interest has been generated amongst overseas manufacturers, particularly the Japanese. Many of the homes can provide clues as to the nature of local businesses as they will be bedecked with products 'acquired' from the workplace.

A village that has a textile factory will display the best curtains for miles around, and all will be remarkably similar. A person who sells door-to-door may notice that every house that he/she visits has the same three piece suite or dining table and chairs. This is an indication that there is a furniture factory in the village.

* * *

A company that I worked for years ago produced coloured steel sheets used for cladding buildings.

The company's main concern was painting the steel before it was 'bent' into the shapes required for the buildings. The paint was delivered in 45 gallon drums, and it was rumoured that one particular worker had managed to get one of these drums off site without detection.

'Well, I d'work at the factory, see, and every day I brought a different piece home with me.'

A few days later, the truth of the matter was out. His entire street had been painted with this paint, known as Juniper Green, a dark coloured green a little like privet, or juniper even.

Every fence, gate, window, door, gutter, drainpipe, shed, and anything else that could be seen had been painted with this stuff. It was a completely matching street. The problem that had been overlooked was that the paint, known in the trade as 'Plastisol', needed to be cured in an oven at hundreds of degrees centigrade before it would 'go off'. You could go back to that street in a hundred years time and the stuff would still be as wet as the day it was brushed on!

So the man who managed to smuggle this drum back to his house, and who must have been for a time, the hero of the street, ended up in extremely bad books with his neighbours. Apparently he wasn't particularly popular with his bosses at work either.

I never knew what became of him, but I would like to think that nothing bad happened as a result of his little venture. I mean, he meant well, didn't he?

*   *   *

Now for some more mining stories…

Dinnertime down the pit was always an exciting affair. The contents of the miners' 'boxes' were a source of great interest, particularly if there had been a darts match in the club or a birthday party the night before. The 'boxes' would be filled with all sorts of titbits; scotch eggs, cocktail sausages, cucumber sandwiches with the crusts cut off etc.

On the whole, the contents were fairly plain and consisted of cheese or ham sandwiches etc.

Rhys and Gareth always sat together for dinner and religiously 'opened' their sandwiches to look inside to see what they had. Gareth would always have a good variety throughout the week, cheese sandwiches on Monday, ham on Tuesday, corned beef on Wednesday etc. Poor old Rhys, on the other hand, had beetroot sandwiches *every* day.

Every dinnertime, Rhys would examine his sandwiches and complain that he had beetroot again. After about six months, Gareth suggested that Rhys spoke to his wife and asked her to give him something else. Rhys thought for a while and said,

'Oh I can't do that, I d'make my own sandwiches.'

Gwilym and Aled always used to compare sandwiches and sometimes used to swap.

One day, Gwilym swapped his ham sandwiches for whatever Aled had, and commented on how nice they were. He asked Aled what the sandwiches were, and Aled told him,

'They'm salmon paste, my missus d'get it from the Cworp.'

The next day, Gwilym was mightily impressed with Aled's sandwiches again and asked what they were. Aled said, 'They'm beef paste, my missus d'get it from Asda.'

The next day, Gwilym was nearly sick when he tasted Aled's sandwiches and said that they were the worst he'd ever tasted. Aled said,

'They'm crab paste, my missus d'get it from the chemist's.'

*   *   *

A travelling salesman walked into a valley pub and asked for a pint of bitter. The landlord poured him a pint and asked him if he was going to buy one for Tudor. The salesman said that he didn't know who Tudor was, so the landlord pointed him out. In the corner was a man, in his eighties. A rugged looking chap with a completely flat head and a cauliflower ear.

The salesman asked the landlord why he should buy Tudor a pint. The landlord said that *everybody* bought Tudor a pint because he was a local hero.

When the salesman asked what he had done, the landlord told of the days when the village had a pit, and one day, there was a serious roof fall. Tudor had saved the lives of the whole shift as he had held up the roof with his head, and stood there until all the men had got out safely. That accounted for his completely flat head. The salesman asked why Tudor had a cauliflower ear as well. The landlord said,

'That's where they hit him with the sledge to wedge him into place.'

*   *   *

Dai, Will, Ieuan and Iolo had all gone to school together. They started in the pit on the same day, all aged 14. They worked together every day until they retired on the same day at the ages of 65.

They went on holidays together, sat together in the club, they were never apart, until the day came that each of them had dreaded, one of the four friends passed away.

It was Dai's funeral and Will, Ieuan and Iolo were paying their last respects at the graveside.

Just as the party were about to leave for the wake, Will took £50 out of his wallet and dropped it onto the top of the coffin.

'I owed him that,' he said, 'It's only fair.'

Ieuan said, 'I owed him £50 as well,' and took £50 out of his wallet and dropped it on top of the coffin. Iolo also admitted to owing Dai £50, but said that he didn't have any cash on him.

He wrote a cheque for £150, placed that on the top of the coffin and pocketed the £100 cash that Will and Ieuan had left.

*   *   *

Dewi came home from the pit one day in a hell of a temper. His wife was very concerned about him and asked him what the trouble was. Dewi said that he'd been working on the coal face and overheard a conversation between two men, one of which was the captain of the rugby team and a bit of a boy for the ladies. The rugby player had told the other man that he'd 'been with' every woman in Dewi's street except one. Dewi's wife thought for a moment and said, 'I expect that'll be that stuck-up bitch from number 37.'

*   *   *

Evan had a nasty bump on the head one day and the pit first-aider suggested that they took him to the hospital for a routine check. All the boys on the shift downed tools and helped the medical team carry Evan through the tunnels back to the Cage which carried the men back to the surface.

When Evan was safely in the cage, the signal was sent to the surface to pull the party up. All the boys on the shift were gathered round wishing him well and giving him a wave. Just as the journey started, one of the lads, Iestyn, rushed to the front of the concerned crowd and yelled, 'Evan!'

Evan raised his head, opened one eye and mumbled, 'What do you want?'

Iestyn replied, 'Can I have your sandwiches?'

*   *   *

Will, Dai and Tom all worked together in the pit. They were best mates, ate together, drank together, went on holidays together – inseparable, they were.

In his spare time, Tom used to go round the clubs as a 'turn'. He had a good tenor voice and used to travel the length and breadth of the valleys entertaining people with renditions of traditional and modern songs, accompanied by backing tapes and a cheap PA system.

One Friday in work, Will asked Dai if he was going in the club for a few pints on the Saturday night. Dai said that he wouldn't be in the club as Tom was singing in a social club in the next valley.

On the following Friday, Will asked Dai if he'd be in the club on Saturday night, and Dai said he wouldn't because Tom was singing in a club in Pontypridd.

As usual, the next Friday, Will asked Dai if he'd be in the club and Dai said he wouldn't because Tom was singing in a club in Treorchy.

Will said to Dai, 'I didn't know you rated Tom as a singer so highly that you spend all your spare time seeing him doing his shows.'

Dai replied, 'It's his wife I'm seeing, not Tom!'

* * *

One day Will lost his hand when he got it caught in the conveyor which took the coal to the surface. He was off work for weeks and was getting used to using his other hand to do all the chores around the house.

Out of the blue, a man from the Health and Safety came round to see him to find out exactly what had happened that caused Will to lose his hand. As Will lived so near to the pit, he suggested that they went underground and Will could demonstrate exactly what happened on that fateful day. The Health and Safety Officer agreed to Will's suggestion.

The pair arrived at the spot where Will had experienced the accident. The Health and Safety Officer made some sketches and Will assumed the position he was in when he lost his hand. He then began to explain,

'So I was standing by here, and I bent down like this, and I stuck my hand out like this and… Oooops, there goes the other one.'

Gwilym had a heavy night on the booze and had such a hangover the next day that he took quite a lot of painkillers. So many in fact, that he didn't even feel it when he lost the index and middle fingers from his right hand in an accident similar to the one that Will experienced. In fact, Gwilym hadn't even noticed they were missing until the end of the shift came and he gestured 'goodbye' to the foreman.

A Nice Mixture

Dai drove for a Cardiff taxi firm, and had taken a booking to pick up an American tourist from Cardiff Airport and take him to Barry. During the flight, the plane had problems and was diverted to Bristol. On landing, the American rang Dai's taxi firm and asked if they wouldn't mind picking him up from Bristol and taking him to Barry from there.

When they were going over the Severn Bridge, the American asked what it was. Dai began to tell the American a bit about the bridge but the American didn't seem to be interested. Instead, he seemed more interested in bragging about his own property. He told Dai that his ranch was split by the Colorado River and he had a bridge twice the size of the Severn Bridge to get from one field to the other, and it only took 6 months to build. In fact, throughout the journey, every landmark they saw, the American had one twice as big, and took half the time to build as the places that Dai pointed out.

When they arrived in Cardiff, they were outside Cardiff Castle at the traffic lights, and once again the American asked what it was. When Dai started to explain, the American interrupted him saying that he had a garage on his land to keep his vehicles in, and funnily enough, it was twice the size of the castle and only took a fortnight to build.

One hundred yards further on, at the next set of lights, the American glanced to his left and spotted the Millennium Stadium. He asked Dai what it was. Dai glanced left, looked at the stadium and said,

'Dunno mate, it wasn't there this morning.'

* * *

Megan and Bryn decided to have a few days out in the summer and take in some of the local scenery. One day they ventured up to the Wye valley and noticed a magnificent building in a very picturesque setting. They stopped to have a look and Bryn went off to buy an ice cream. When he came back, he'd picked up a pamphlet which told the story of the building. 'Apparently, this place is called Tintern Abbey,' he said to Megan.

They were so impressed that they decided to do the guided tour, and when they got back in the car, they were overwhelmed with the size of the place and the magnificent stonework that the building contained.

As they were pulling out of the car park, Megan turned to Bryn and said, 'I tell you what luv, we'll come back yer again when they've got the roof on and finished it off tidy shall we?'

* * *

Geraint got a job driving for the local timber yards. He turned up for his first shift and the boss told him to take a lorry load of wood to Birmingham. The boss went into the office to get the paperwork for the delivery, and when he got back to the yard, discovered that Geraint had already driven off and was on his way.

Four hours later, he arrived in Wrexham. He stopped and asked a passer-by if this was Birmingham. The passer-by told him that he was in Wrexham and that Birmingham was a long way south of where he was at the moment.

Two hours later, he pulled up in Cardigan and asked a passer-by if he was in Birmingham. The passer-by told him he was in Cardigan and told him that he needed to go east to get to Birmingham. Five hours later, Geraint pulled up in Merthyr Tydfil and asked a passer-by if this was Birmingham.

Six days later, Geraint finally arrived at his destination. He stopped right outside the Bullring and asked a passer-by if this was Birmingham. When the passer-by told him he was in Birmingham, Geraint said, 'Thank God for that! Where do you want this wood?'

*   *   *

Rhodri and Dewi were having such a good time in town one night that they forgot to leave the pub in time to catch the last bus back to their valley. They decided that they would have to walk home as they couldn't get a taxi for at least three hours.

They had only been walking for five minutes when they found themselves outside the bus depot. Rhodri could drive a bus as he had a PSV licence, and between them they decided to steal a bus and Rhodri would drive them home.

So, with Dewi acting as lookout, Rhodri climbed over the wall to steal a bus.

Dewi could hear all sorts of noises coming from the depot. He heard Rhodri starting a bus and heard him reverse it, then a crash. Then he heard another bus start up, and another crash. Then another, and then another. After an hour, Rhodri chugged out of the depot in a bus that was covered in dents and had bits hanging off it.

When Dewi got on the bus he said,

'What have you been doing? You must've smashed up every bus in there!'

Rhodri replied,

'Aye, the trouble was, our bus was right up the back.'

*   *   *

Dai and Iolo went to Cardiff shopping one day and decided to call into a restaurant for something to eat. The place was a bit posh, and they were treated like royalty by the staff.

Dai and Iolo checked out the menu for sausage, egg and chips and pie, beans and chips (which was their usual order) and everything was in French!

According to the menu, all dishes came with rice, salad or choice of potato.

They politely asked the waitress to explain the terms on the menu and she was very helpful. Dai ordered a chicken dish with rice and Iolo ordered a fancy steak.

The waitress turned to Iolo and asked him if he'd like to make his choice of potato.

Iolo leaned back in his seat and said,

'Aye, go on then luv, fetch 'em over by yer – let's have a look at 'em.'

*   *   *

Dai went to the chemist's to get something for a chesty cough. There was a spate of chesty coughs going round and the chemist had run out of the appropriate medicine.

Dai asked him if he could make something up for him.

The chemist said, 'Mick Jagger was in here earlier.'

Dai replied, 'Was he really?'

The chemist retorted, 'No, I just made that up for you.'

*   *   *

Finally, a tale of disillusionment…

A young lad was walking his dog on the mountainside when he spied an old man sitting on a bench, surveying the valley with a forlorn look on his face. He sat by the man and asked him if he was OK. The man looked at the young lad, and smiled. Then with a tear in his eye, he told a strange story.

'Well you see m'boy, I'm coming to the end of my life. I d'come up yer most days to look at the valley and think about all the things what I have done for this community and all the things what I achieved since I was put on this Earth.

I was the first boy from this valley to go to Oxford, and I came out of there in 1953 with a first-class honours degree. I was the hero of the valley I was. People came from miles around to talk to me about their problems. I was respected throughout these valleys and I never charged no-one a penny for giving advice. And do they call me 'Dai the Philanthropist'? No! Do they Hell!

In 1962, the old bridge fell down. See that bridge over the river there boy? I designed and built that myself. Been there for over 40 years it has. The villagers would have had to take a 25-mile bus ride to get to the other side of that river if it hadn't been for me. Been there for 40 years it has. Aye, that bridge has saved a lot of people a lot of trouble. And do they call me 'Dai the Engineer'? No! Do they Hell!

See that farm over there on the opposite mountain boy? You won't remember it, but that used to be a barren wasteland. I decided to use that land to produce top quality food for the people of these valleys. I dug the soil from the one side of the mountain with my bare hands. I built all the dry stone walls, planted magnificent orchards and fields full of the best vegetables and bred the biggest and best livestock in Europe.

I provided the best grub to all these valleys for over 30 years, and only charged a fraction of what it would cost them in these supermarkets.

And do they call me 'Dai the Farmer'? No! Do they Hell!

One sheep, that's all it was, one bloody sheep!'

Heard in Public Places

This section deals with some strange things that have been said in the pubs, clubs, supermarkets and any other establishments that are frequented by people in the valleys.

We know what they meant to say, but it came out a bit awry, as you can see.

Some words do not actually exist, so to ease the reading process, they have been spelt phonetically to capture the beauty of the language…

'It was the best night I've ever had in my life, for a long time.'

'He gave me the letter and it took me half an hour to siphon it out.'
(decipher it)

'I've forgotten to feed the turpentines.' (terrapins)

'Your phone bill must be absolutely gastronomic.'

'He can play darts with either hand, he's bisexual.'

'I read that the Elan Valley is one of the most pitcherskew places in Britain.'

'When's the baby due?'
'Christmas.'
'This Christmas?'

'There's too much foreplay in this gearstick.'

'I've had my back passage painted in Mongolia.' (magnolia)

'All you need now is a pelvis over that window.'

'Those darts are not bad for six quid a pair.'

'We'll have to put the anus on him to do it.' (onus)

'I've only got two pairs of hands.'

'Where were you going the other day when I saw you coming back?'

'Get me a new iron from down the shops.'
'Steam?'
'No, electric you idiot!'

'If I had to count them on my fingers, I'd have to take my shoes off.'

'That's another bow to your arrow.'

'I'm running around like a chicken without his head off.'

'This guy bit his ear, and he was HGV positive.'

'We went to France on the aerosol.'

'Just because I've got the gloves on it doesn't mean I'm going to wear them.'

'If I won the lottery, I'd fly off to the nearest faraway place.'

'I'm sure there's an alligator somewhere in this pub, and if you see him, let me know!'

'Allegations have been made that I have had my fingers in the till, allegations have been made that I've been fiddling the tote, allegations have been made that I've been drinking the stock, and if I find out who the alligator is, there'll be murder!'

'Hell hath no fury like a woman spermed.'

'I was going to have my eyes tested today but they were shut.'

'I like the old Rod Stewart, when he was younger.'

'I don't know much about golf,
I don't even know how to hold the caddy.'

'One man's meat isn't everyone's cup of tea.'

'You three are a right pair if ever I saw one.'

'It's about time they put their foot down with a firm hand.'

'This is happening 99.9 times out of ten!'

'That kestrel must have eyes like a hawk.'

'If you've still got that leg on Monday you want to take it to the doctors.'

'Do you want your afters now or after?'

'She's had more phantom pregnancies than the Phantom of the Opera.'

'We had a good night last night at the Kamikaze evening.' (karaoke)

'The trouble with rats is they breed like rabbits.'

'I'll spell it out for you, that's P for Percy and N for knackered.'

'They don't make those old films any more do they?'

'I think he's a bit ABCD.' (AC/DC)

'I've been saying that for a long time but I kept my mouth shut.'

'My mother can use both hands equally well, she's amphibious you know.'

'You are a boiled sprat!'

'If you do't start behaving yourself, you'll be seeing the back of my fin, m'boy!'

'Hands up all those that didn't have an Easter egg for Christmas.'

'She's a lot better, she's having an autopsy next week.' (biopsy)

'I'm thinking of getting rid of these socks. They're on their last legs.'

'Timber doesn't grow on trees you know!'

'A virgin wood is where the hand of man has never trod.'

'What did you call him John for? Every Tom, Dick or Harry's called John!'

'This marks the end of a long life and an even longer career.'

'I'm going into this meeting, and I'm going to cause absolute termite.' (turmoil)

'I'm sorry. That is out of my due restriction.' (jurisdiction)

'So, where you live it's only a five minute walk to where you work, is it?'
'Aye, and if I run, it's only a two minute walk.'

'Now I'm right up a gum tree without a paddle.'

'She's not too clever on her feet these days. She has to go round on a strimmer.'

'He stopped breathing so they gave him artificial insemination.'

'Have a listen to this CD. It's a copulation album of rock anthems.'
(compilation)

'His father was born in Cardiff, so he was illegible to play for Wales.'

'I've been up and down these stairs more times than a yo-yo today!'

'And we've all passed a lot of water under the bridge since then.'

'We're going on a mystery trip in the morning.'
'Really? Where to?'

'The powers to be have minds that boggle passed everyone else's.'

'I'm not trying to take anything away from you to any extent or level, but he's got me over a barrel and I can't get out of it.'

'I'm going to send her some flowers through Interpol.'

'Bonjour, Madame. Please accept these as a token of my lurve!'

'He was conspicuous by his lack of absence.'

'We're both thinking the same way, but going about it in reverse.'

'It was like opening Tandoori's Box.'

'You can't tar every brush with one nutter.'

'Hitler tried those tactics with the desert rats and ended up with a desert fox.'

'This is a case of the chicken not knowing what the egg is doing.'

'The right hand is saying one thing and the left hand saying the other, and I'm stuck in the middle like a pig's purse.'

'Your hair on the back of your head is sticking up like a dog's hind leg.'

'I don't want anything flashy, just a normal, bog-standard toilet.'

'If you wake up with a hangover, have another pint straightaway. It's like the hair off another dog's back.'

'Before my husband died my lawn was like a billiard ball.'

'I've got to call into the Chemist's to get my description.'

'Now the winter is coming on, I'll have to get some deep freeze to put in the car.'

'Oooh, they was great, them flamingoes! It was like poultry in motion.'

'Those flamingo dancers were absolutely brilliant.'

'I notice that on Sundays they have the 'Weather for Farmers' on the radio. Is that any different to the weather we have?'

'A bottle of your finest Bowjollis please.' (Beaujolais)
'I can see you know your wine sir.'
'Yes, I do consider myself to be a bit of a courvoissier.' (Connisseur)

'And this woman, who was about eighteen months pregnant, walked in.'

'This is a pleasant conversation for a lunchtime!'
'If you think this is bad, it's a good job you weren't here before you got back!'

'We're going to the Bahamas for our holidays this year.'
'Which one?'
'All of 'em.'

'Everything's hoikey doikey again now.' (hunky dory)

'She had twins - a boy and a girl.'
'Identical?'

'I ought to go to his funeral really, especially as I missed the last one.'

'Why don't you get one of those dildo rails put up? They look quite nice.' (dado)

'You two are like the three stooges.'

'Put the numbers in a bag and draw them out of a hat.'

'He'd been drinking all day and he came home abbreviated.' (inebriated)

'Hopefully there's a silver lining at the end of the tunnel.'

'I expect he'll be making a beehive for her now.' (beeline)

'You must think I came up the river on a pushbike.'

'Those fish in my tank are getting pretty thin on the ground.'

'It's over to you, Bob!'

'The police threw an accordion around the house.' (cordon)

'Are you going to Wally's Bonfire Night party?'
'When is it?'

'Would you like an aperteefer before we eat?' (aperitif)

'I hope there's a buffet laid on at this party. I'm absolutely ravishing.' (ravenous)

'A man died again on the squash court yesterday.'

'That Les Routier must be worth a fortune. He's got hotels all over France.'

'I've been having some funny phone calls lately, so I'm going hysterectomy.' (ex-directory)

'I'll put it in my diary now before I forget it… Now, when's Christmas?'

'I'm getting too old for this.'
'What're you on about? I'm older than you!'
'Aye, but only in years.'

'I think we may be barking up the wrong trouser leg here.'

'I just can't believe the lies you've been coming out with lately.'

'He's got a vase from the mink dysentery.' (ming dynasty)

'He couldn't go to the toilet properly, so he had to have a cafeteria fitted.'

'I hit the ball with all the venison I could muster.' (venom)

'Tidy shot! It'll take two good hits to get up that hill in three today.'

'She died of Anorexia Mitsibushi.' (nervosa)

'Have you ever seen 'Wildlife on David Attenborough'?'

'It'll look good with a lick of paint here and there and a bit of Aztec on the ceiling.' (artex)

'Don't mention gout to me. It's like toothache in your foot.'

'I wasn't born under a roseberry bush.'

'We've been down to MI5 to have a look at some carpet.'

'He's always mispronounciating things wrong.'

'He bent the ball round the goalkeeper like a cucumber.'

'I haven't done it yet. I haven't had two minutes to rub together.'

'They showed an operation on the telly last night and you could see all this guy's intesticles.'

'I don't know whether it's metric or impartial.'

'It'll be a game of three halves.'

'You're trying to make a sow's ear out of a pig's purse.'

'It gets late early round here, doesn't it?'

'Thank you madam. They'll be ready Thursday if you want to pick them up then.'

'I'm going to have my ears pierced. Will they do it while you wait?'

'I deny that flatulently!'

'Latin is a completely dead language.'
'Not if you come from Latvia it isn't!'

'He hasn't been hurt by that tackle. You watch, as soon as the free-kick is taken, he'll be running around like a new born baby.'

'Even if I could have understood him, I wouldn't have known what he was on about.'

'Even if you get it wrong, you've got a fifty-fifty chance of getting it right.'

'What type of dog is Snoopy, anyway?'
'A Dalmatian.'
'I thought Fred Bassett was a Dalmatian.'
'Don't be stupid, Fred Bassett is a Beagle!'

'With mosquitos, the worst are the pregnant females.'
'What about the pregnant males?'

'That coconut oil was useless for my sunburn. It was so horrible, I had to spit it out after the first mouthful.'

'My missus is in hospital getting over a vasectomy.'

'My cousin just had a baby.'
'What did she have?'
'Dunno, it was either a boy or a girl.'

'You are not using me as a hamster to try your home made wine out on.' (guinea pig)

'I'm worried about our Julie – the only greens I can get her to eat is carrots.'

'Don't worry about the dark. Your eyes will soon accumulate.'

'Just a few more eyes and I should be able to see where I'm going!'

'Paul has gone to the psychiatrists with his pelvic.'
(physiotherapist - pelvis)

'The trouble with him is that he spends 75% of his time talking, 50% wasting time, 20% in the toilet and only 10% doing what he's supposed to be doing.'

'What's Fred's surname?'
'Fred who?'

'Those weeds need to be ridiculed as soon as possible.' (eradicated)

'Is that a real forged note?'

'That goldfish looks as though it's on its last legs.'

'We're off to celebrate VD Day.'

'He always opens his mouth before he says anything.'

'What are you hoping to get for your house?'
'Between twelve thousand and whatever I can get for it.'

'He lost seven fingers!'
'All off the same hand?'

'There was a lot of snue gliffers hanging around at the bus station.'
(glue sniffers)

'Watch out for that sentiment in the bottom of your wine glass.'
(sediment)

'Go on, son, take it. Take it all! And there's more where that came from. Just say the word!'

'He's generous to a tree.'

'If my mother was alive today, she'd have been dead for twenty years.'

'Is this the Cuppa Soup with the crispy cretins?' (croutons)

'Many of the early Laurel and Hardy films were silent.'
'A lot of the early Goon Show radio broadcasts were silent as well, weren't they?'
'I dunno. I never heard any of them.'

'I've decided to go celebus.' (celibate)

'My father bought a car, the same as the last one he had.'
'Is it an estate like the other one?'
'Yes, but he's having this one done up.'

'Have you got any Cajun music?'
'Yes, what occasion do you want it for?'

'It's happened several times in the past and it's still going on
in this day and age, but let's hope that in the future
it'll be a thing of the past.'

'All I have to do is flatter my eyelids at him.'

'They're making Cardiff into one big shopping prefix.' (precinct)

Final Thoughts

The Tom Jones Connection

It would not be a good idea to visit all the valleys here and to discuss their particular traits because it could be an endless task. This has been intended as a short guide to the language and to highlight some very common features which should enable the visitor to 'get by' in the valleys. I thought it would be a good idea to mention one very important and sinister anomaly that a visitor will need to be prepared for if he/she ever encounters someone from Pontypridd:

Over the years I have met people from Pontypridd, about twenty in all, and I have noticed something which is exclusive to them. It will happen not long after you start talking to them. The subject of Tom Jones will crop up. On average, this happens within the first minute of the start of the conversation, and it will always be brought up by the Pontypriddian.

Phrases to watch out for are:

'Of course, Tommy Woodward is his *real* name.'

'Oh aye, went to school with him, sat next to him I did.'

'Lived next door to him… my mother still does!'

'He used to deliver papers to our house.'

'He got chucked out of our Social Club for being crap.'

'Used to go out with his sister.'

'Always pops in our house with something for our mam when he d'come home.'

After speaking to a Pontypriddian I always have some unanswered questions.

(1) How long was Tom Jones in school? The ages of the twenty or so people that I have spoken to, that sat next to him in school, range from nineteen to seventy nine. Has he actually left school yet?

(2) Would it be possible to have a look at an aerial photograph of Tom's house? When you consider that the same twenty-odd people who sat by him in school used to live next door to him – and their mothers still do – then this suggests that Tom's house must look like a huge twenty-sided 50p piece from above, with all these little houses attached to each of the sides

It's all very strange.

I'll tell you what's even stranger, out of all Tom Jones's next door neighbours, I've met them all!

Either that or some of them have been telling porkies.

No, they wouldn't do that.

Would they?

Summing up

Now that you've had an introduction to the art of 'talking valley', do you think that you'd be able to get by? You will certainly be able to converse with the locals a lot easier, and, if you stick to the general rules of grammar described here, you will make yourself understood better. You may even, depending on how adaptable you are, be able to pass yourself off as a valley person.

Visiting the valleys will not be such a daunting prospect for you now, you may even consider selling up and moving in!

This book is not only useful for those who intend spending time in the valleys, it can also be a vital reference for those who live at seaside resorts or other places that are visited by holiday makers. Valley people go on holidays to resorts throughout the UK and abroad and they will talk 'pure valley' for the duration of their stays.

If you own a guest house or shop, you will come into contact with this language and it is important that you are able to understand requests for goods fairly quickly, as a valley person will often get impatient after the third 'Pardon?' and leave your premises without buying anything.

Generally, groups of valley people stick together when in this environment and will not generally stray away from their group. Valley people who meet other valley people whilst on holiday will accept these into their own group and regard them as lifelong friends. The first thing that will draw these people together will be the language, usually overheard in shops and queues, and they will realise that another valley person is at large. The initial contact will be made through a phrase such as, 'Where are you from then?'

When their roots have been fully established, they will look for a link, no matter how tenuous, to convince themselves that they really *did* know each other all their lives even though they only actually met about ten minutes earlier. This link could be someone that they all know, a pub that they've all been to, or in extreme cases, a rugby International at the Millennium Stadium that they all attended. This will be enough to form the bond to keep them together for the whole of the holiday.

Of course, they will never ever get in contact with each other when they get home, and will probably tell all their friends about the 'dickheads' they met on holidays and how they hope that they never bump into them again.

This has been a short introduction to valley life and its language. I hope that you have enjoyed it and that you will venture into the hills to witness the culture and scenery for yourselves. The valley people have long been misunderstood and ridiculed by those who 'speak proper like', but humour is always present whether intentional or otherwise.

Why not give us a visit and see for yourselves?